Bird Arsonist

Arsc

Bird Arsonist

Gary Barwin
& Tom Prime

VANCOUVER I NEW STAR BOOKS I 2022

NEW STAR BOOKS LTD

No. 107–3477 Commercial St, Vancouver, BC V5N 4E8 CANADA

1574 Gulf Road, No. 1517 Point Roberts, WA 98281 USA

newstarbooks.com · info@newstarbooks.com

The publisher acknowledges the financial support of the Canada Council for the Arts,
the British Columbia Arts Council, and the Government of Canada.
Nous reconnaissons l'appui financier du gouvernement du Canada.

Funded by the
Government
of Canada

Canada

Canada Council   Conseil des arts
for the Arts   du Canada

BRITISH COLUMBIA
ARTS COUNCIL

BRITISH
COLUMBIA

Supported by the Province of British Columbia

Cataloguing information for this book is available from Library
and Archives Canada, www.collectionscanada.gc.ca.
ISBN: 9781554201853

Edited by Donato Mancini
Cover design by Oliver McPartlin
Typeset by New Star Books
Printed and bound in Canada by Imprimerie Gauvin, Gatineau, QC

First printing February 2022

17:15:54 From ███████████ to ██████████
Hugh Strigose
17:19:05 From ███████████ to ██████████
3D-Printed Beak

I tell this tale with broken mouth
my ravaged clock

with stallion teeth
o quaggy baby with guns of bone

makingrittedrear. Buz| zing hapless yout| hling freezer. frozen | grinululate. masectomillitant. ion

shroudbereft outer-tin| s milked of granul| ar muscle chalk.| bungled retrospectively asterisk

shaped hydrogen ostr| ich bea|ked nostal| giamower. greeted fowl at in-peeled film lash.

{miresc   ess draped in h| ospital c| ur| tains. ill-lit in | the circumambience.

meaning   allowb| reather harpmolar| bu| rntdrizzler babysky clocksmoke deathpi}zzle

l ectomy ur ectomy & | rather otomy than | thi| s victorious grammar atomy

nodule

:cubicle curtain

nodule

cubicle curtain:

l ectomy ur ectomy & | rather otomy than | thi| s victorious grammar atomy

meaning   allowb| reather harpmolar| bu| rntdrizzler babysky clocksmoke deathpi}zzle

{miresc   ess draped in h| ospital c| ur| tains. ill-lit in | the circumambience.

shaped hydrogen ostr| ich bea|ked nostal| giamower. greeted fowl at in-peeled film lash.

shroudbereft outer-tin| s milked of granul| ar muscle chalk.| bungled retrospectively asterisk

makingrittedrear. Buz| zing hapless yout| hling freezer. frozen | grinululate. masectomillitant. ion

CONTENTS

IV. THE ADRENAL WHALE

V. FAIR SEMIRAMIS

VI. NIBBLING TITHES

ACKNOWLEDGEMENTS

I. CLOUD-PUNCHED

bird arsonist: surgery smell and super-glue spray of eyes

Null Island

dreamer of roses, hairy with rainguns
the biosphere is calling. funds
are going to survive spacetime
stag against eliminated text

I can no longer afford to want

Blink

oloooooooo
oloooooooo

I say and do not protein

oloooooooo
oloooooooo

it helios

*

oloooooooo
oloooooooo

canned island

oloooooooo
oloooooooo

DNA belly shack

Où

sky was delicious and vibrated   a body
   no different than   opening
"was I names?"

"braceleting outside   babies"

One Day I'll Speak

blue-eyed flip-phones, sawtoothed spineclip, spindle needlebox

spatchcock

II. EQUINOX OF THE REAPER

bird arsonist: bilious nerve-endings not without nymph-fish

1.

"

Having a bear in one's dream is to have a bicycle. Frankly "the" is oversharing. It is correct   to be frightened. Neither undertake, write, nor publish.

Reapers will speak impressionably, the casing of their brains, a
                                         lighthouse,
propose to become the nervous pal of shoulders.

I would not lose any of the milquetoast pasture of fleshy pebble blue inhale   these waves.

2.

A word fitly spoken is what the sky looks like to a wheel broken near your sister's child.

And let me add "this," the excellent library of wings. I perceive boulders as small stones.

Lullaby-sparrow may wren the knot   fob-fitters with weapons of dew. I shall stay by the
windscreen jibe   bones defy whereupon   they shrink.

III. NEUROTIC MIDDEN

I now am not the pointer's dimpled now; if it be not mouth

GAMMABATH

Prior Tongues

ate their hot facepalm
the hot-wired egg therein

I ruddied
bandaged, the midnight feed-hole
compression bed
        furtive, boiled as glands

*

the tide

unable to breathe
        breathing
unable to breathe

Nid Mizzle

livid doughnut fish, thin rain-wrapped blunder-furniture

E _{(H η}

[somethinginthethetetragrammaton]

radio

chug the demarcated value bin

twinlight_{shullamite}tap_{djinn}eidetic^{vernalickular}ear

thought
sunk

Burning with Scissors

ruling moth-fissure   brindled
       sine-tissue
money lobed
             sternumgrates

       the thrown "ask"

pixis flustered derivatives therein glummingulg happifying groal, erstwhile longswordained glitches uncouth addendum. ailing non-sequestered astral-bucket, singe green from retinal expansion back, kind as this scoured funneling wedges, the petrichor are a blood ironness.

pulsates radially, amplitude

H

h

the magellanic clouds hinge to

cot(h)fin-shaped gravity dovetails, lifting the grease skiff ———— taciturn

h   the Puerile thought

echtramadolmimesis

H

ere the mountaininternal rain like a coast₂

the chest ghosts the fingers , eyes like fawns
in opalescence and nostaglight. Pyrites of the radial.
Iris hunters of the prism. All deaths seen at once
lose their colour

)

Birdoxy

honey lip-shod
newly
    parent the seas
suckle the wizardly
morning lag

oOoOoOoOoOoOoOoOoOoOoȯooOooooOooooOoOoOoOoOoOoOoO
oOooooOooooOroOOonOoOooonionOooggleOnitsOooooOooooo
OoOoOiloOoOOOOntologicOooOoooOoulipOooobservOverservo
OoooOooooOoOoOoOoOooooOooooOooooOoOoOoOoOoOoOo
OrdinantoOoOoOoOoOoOpenOpenOpenOpalescenOooOooooO-
falooooooooooooooooOotoothlopmoOooomegachurchOo
O..O..O..O..O..O..O..O..OO..O..O..OO..O..O..OO..O..O..OO..O..O
..OO..O..O..OO..O..O..OO..O..O

0O0O0O0O0O0O0O0O0O0O0O0O0O^{int t_[8]={1,0,1,1,1,2,2,1};}

int t_90[8]={0,1,1,0,1,1,2,1};

int t_180[8]={0,1,1,0,1,1,1,2};

int t_270[8]={0,1,1,1,1,2,2,1};

O0O0O0O0O0O0O0O0O0O0O0O0O0O0O0O0O0O0O0O0O0O0O0O0O
oooóoœoooöooooôoooooooooòooooooóoœoooöooooôoooooooooòooooooo
óoœoooöooooôooooooooò
0O0O0O0O0O0O0O0O0O0O0O0O0O0O0O0O0O0O0O0O0O0O0O0O0O
0O0O0O0O0O0O0O0O0O0O0O0O0O0O0O0O0O

oooóoœoooöooooôoooooooooòooooooóoœoooöooooôoooooooooòooooooo
óoœoooöooooôoooooooooò0O0O0O0O0O0O0O0O0O0O0O0O0O0O0O0O0O0O0O0
O0O0O0O0O0O0O0O0O0O0O0O0O0O0O0O0O0O0O0O

oooóoœoooöooooôoooooooooòooooooóoœoooöooooôoooooooooòooooooo
óoœoooöooooôooooooooò

Burning my Ox like Lexical Bones

blood limits moss-snow patches
the doily housed
bugfixes   pink antiquity

deer heat through splatter
trout-coloured
"would"
seed the ligneous bellows

grass gasps   our eyes

Ands My Widow

her leafed
        the driver falls
a frog, o baleful
monoglyph

tuskless "has"

Fraught He Looks in Heaven for Bluebells

he who does not know cradle
laughter-like icicle

Stars Rubbing

                        flooded   angels pretend you
aren't
shipping addresses   a canal's smoke neighbourhood

   let's stalk "about"

Higgs Boson arms   feet with hand... ... ...
... ...   footsoldiers with the
palace
     outh.
Le...   ...n tooled for a little
...   t never late   ...
capital sm. The feet, as long as the feet   ...
Topscore co...   ... mouth s...
... ...   abutment; ...
To the mouth, ...   good for polka   ...ed appliances.
       oral hygiene   highscore   ...   walking
Abrasion o...   A weapon, ...   breathes.

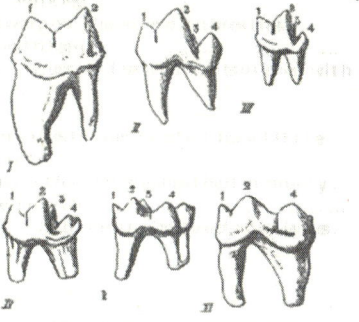

Abrasion of polka. A ...
Higgs Boson arms their feet ...   ...th
the palace of the open
mouth
Let's imagine Boss to be a...
puppy to market but never ...
capital sm. The feet, a...
Topscore continuation the the ...

IV. THE ADRENAL WHALE

blazon-mouthed tax-free "here"

or tender-glove radium
palanquin anklet

Subcutaneous Midden

rescinded peregrine fingers
semi-haemorrhaging
forehead-lipped lake

a fucktschrift post-vole
cerulean herd

Love is a Bald Noodling of Translators:

o

Love is Noodling a Bald of Translators

Breathing is a Gash from Outside the Lungs

sidereal sleep-hatchet
closets lesions   burrowed cinders
grin like throat   slips
fossils

                    we say we mean
                              clouds as wavelengths
                    seeded "of"

A Lake like Forest Clot Crumpled Sandwich Bags

Did you not already give frowning brows?[1]

Testimony where we recollect hair.[2]

Too many walked about, punitive with sleeping bags in the Zephyr-filled[3] baby street. As furtive as they were waxwing, they have burnt illegal. Crimpled. Disc-like. Sorrowful.

If we were chipped in a stimp then bevelled.

Name meadow: I ate my Zaqqum[4].

Speaking pinions arc-welded under the birdstream. Tenderstone.

The fog lathed nipped blades xs petrified chicken. I wade stupid climax.

Sleeping[5] is a tree sheathed in money.

---

[1] Yeah, I don't squirrel a Gematria craquelure.

[2] I spoke to photoshopped knees.

[3] "Buy my 'are' knives."

[4] These are slick pieces of O.

[5] $4.76.

Dibble Wing

parentheses mountains

the debt horizon brailles
crow. I am here   to shoot
the bruise-shaped
smoke

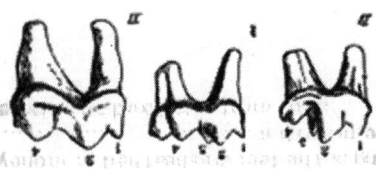

M

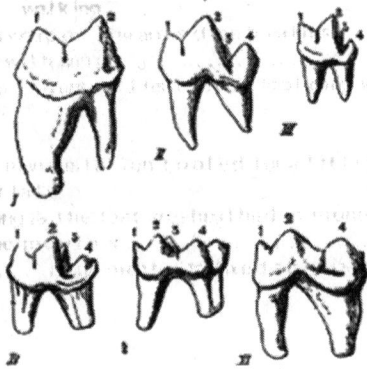

...with

...

et's imagine it's also to be a house ... pooled to a little
iggy to market but never ...
pital ... The first as I ... is the ... ... that had ... many
opscon ... commodit ... the ...

V. FAIR SEMIRAMIS

birth is boustrophedon except when it birds birthmarks
deadlines the spacesuit in doors.

Fair Semiramis

When the writer whispers
the wound fills with kindling.
                              —Anonymous

1.
four-bird tree grows an earthquake
in the garden, a dimpled plastic fan
boat screechings   you're almost
cigarettes

window the doughlight
no platelet on which to land
no writer filled with stitch

ok, so:
          the rabbit mouthed lotus
seedheadholeshead

                              blue dwarf
the dog's wistful fields
arrhythmic
ionic feet or voltaic spondees
teeth caged in erotic Manhattan

we made a box of streetlight
sagged in Travel Lodge pool

I don't remember what a dimple of
strangle marks said
a wreath from the dog's phonemes
gills   a fan
an incubator taxi, cistern

2.

megaphone exit ramps
home the milk-inked fervour

pushworm spindle phlegm
the cloven dissent-lark

3.

vacation for a week
the pin feathers of Jim's wheel
lopsided darkness
the push-cart dartboard
stentorian

grinning a ~~slit~~ ~~fire~~

4.

kids' murky roof
grimace
a raindug foxhole

      shiver dress
      dragged from blankie
miser braids

5.
lips of little milk
coked by skies

coupon gutted
semi-glee
syringe of baby

6.
US fin-proud
tombstone crypto
that blush crimped
lemon-blade

Alphagetti skinhole
still-housed a mega-church
crusty Hubble
the dictionary purrs
beards

VI.
NIBBLING
TITHES

cattle prod light beneath the nectar bowl, thought   a knack for threading honey

Binge-armoured Coruscated

in spring, a captain is
here with nibbling tithes

overgowned in dead
ferns   resuscitations
a bridge of marmosets in the no
reside in dorsal

a co-pilot teflon sift-mask

workers lament the fission
tube-sow   an internal
review

I remember when death began
donating babies to the government

I, a friend of dew
and bereavements
dowsed in prickle rain

was I blurred therein
does prickle rain?

Warble-hum

ah trans-fat microwave

the frontal-lobe
huge as mice
grief missile

poultice Edie Sedgwick lebensraum orbicular hen necks
poultice wig-skull defibrillated debt-magnet
poultice ultrathin pantomime

o babies soft as guns
babies soft as guns

Strait of Messina Strap-on

hadron-stippled politicians
conditioner-egg cave
children

quail-marbled wet jaw
inwardly stretched
the quasi squiff
archive

Bathypelagic Grips

obit-shaped narwhal
glister horn   linear pump
the shank eye

$$Q = \underline{moribund*2(petrichor)}$$
pending sonnet

doves
doves

$$Borb = \underline{Retrovirus= sloop(boon)egret2}$$
Torporbrb, *LOL(milky fire!) ¯_(ツ)_/¯

Quaggy Baby

dent be coal-pit
my corrupt .gif
seamless heaps of silver-ships
antipodes
the fridge of Jeremiads

oh outdated minivan
robot's jowl-sails
whip-kept the widow
abacus

Anacrusis Granule

plumed apotheosis
      a muscly encloakment
oracles brokered   bereft, states
the accordion's sieve-musth
one could marry
      the surface of inadvertent
lake

Acknowledgements

17:21:56 From Tom Prime to Everyone:
Dean Fouilloy, Beyorn Wig M.A. R-Tamrip. Corpse
and Beans, Saint Geraud.

17:22:19 From Gary Barwin (he/him) to Everyone:
Amp Writing Marr-Eboy.

17:23:38 From Gary Barwin (he/him) to Everyone:
IMMY GRAB POWERTRAIN

17:24:47 From Tom Prime to Everyone:
cover designer Oliver McPartlin,
editors Vlad Cristache, Rolf Maurer,
and designer Melissa Swann

17:25:01 From Gary Barwin (he/him) to Everyone:
Donato Mancini for invaluable ret chainsaw editing

17:25:04 From Gary Barwin (he/him) to Everyone:
Felix Bernstein for the thoughtful words

17:25:09 From Tom Prime to Everyone:
Jonathan Ball like, wise

17:28:10 From Gary Barwin (he/him) to Everyone:
Cpt B. Garwin, Volunteer Avian Hose Company of

17:28:21 From Tom Prime to Everyone:
Rom Twime for the self-exculpation.

17:28:27 From Gary Barwin (he/him) to Everyone:
Regretsville

17:29:45 From Gary Barwin (he/him) to Everyone:
Volunteer Avian Incunabulum Hose

17:31:29 From Gary Barwin (he/him) to Everyone:

Some of the work in *Bird Arsonist* was first published
(in a different form) in [two chapbooks] from serif of nottingham:
Equinox of the Reaper and Birds are the Birthmarks of Flight

17:31:58 From Tom Prime to Everyone:

Dianetics: the Modern Science of Mental Health (1950)

17:33:20 From Gary Barwin (he/him) to Everyone:

& appeared in the video *Fair Semiramis* (created for Poetry London);

17:34:01 From Tom Prime to Everyone:

it's here: https://youtu.be/dKZkghKu38E

17:35:17 From Gary Barwin (he/him) to Everyone:

& supporters of public funding for the arts